NUMBER LINES
How Far to the Car?

Based on the Math Monsters™ public television series, developed in cooperation with the National Council of Teachers of Mathematics (NCTM).

by John Burstein

Reading consultant: Susan Nations, M.Ed., author/literacy coach/consultant

Math curriculum consultants: Marti Wolfe, M.Ed., teacher/presenter; Kristi Hardi-Gilson, B.A., teacher/presenter

WEEKLY WR READER®
EARLY LEARNING LIBRARY

Please visit our web site at: **www.earlyliteracy.cc**
For a free color catalog describing Weekly Reader® Early Learning Library's list
of high-quality books, call 1-877-445-5824 (USA) or 1-800-387-3178 (Canada).
Weekly Reader® Early Learning Library's fax: (414) 336-0164.

Library of Congress Cataloging-in-Publication Data

Burstein, John.
    Number lines: how far to the car? / by John Burstein.
       p. cm. — (Math monsters)
    Summary: The four monsters set up number signs along Monster Town Road
to help Multiplex find cars when they break down.
    ISBN 0-8368-3815-7 (lib. bdg.)
    ISBN 0-8368-3830-0 (softcover)
    1. Number line—Juvenile literature.   2. Number concept—Juvenile literature.
[1. Number line.   2. Number concept.]   I. Title.
QA141.15.B864   2003
513—dc21   2003045043

This edition first published in 2004 by
Weekly Reader® Early Learning Library
330 West Olive Street, Suite 100
Milwaukee, WI 53212 USA

Text and artwork copyright © 2004 by Slim Goodbody Corp. (www.slimgoodbody.com).
This edition copyright © 2004 by Weekly Reader® Early Learning Library.

Original Math Monsters™ animation: Destiny Images
Art direction, cover design, and page layout: Tammy Gruenewald
Editor: JoAnn Early Macken

Printed in the United States of America

1 2 3 4 5 6 7 8 9 07 06 05 04 03

You can enrich children's mathematical experiences by working with
them as they tackle the Corner Questions in this book. Create
a special notebook for recording their mathematical ideas.

Number Lines and Math

Number lines are valuable tools for young mathematicians. Number
lines are often used in the early grades for a variety of purposes,
including counting, addition, and subtraction.

Meet the Math Monsters

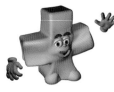

ADDISON

Addison thinks
math is fun.
"I solve problems
one by one."

Mina flies
from here to there.
"I look for answers
everywhere."

MINA

MULTIPLEX

Multiplex
sure loves to laugh.
"Both my heads
have fun with math."

Split is friendly
as can be.
"If you need help,
then count on me."

SPLIT

We're glad you want to take a look
at the story in our book.

We know that as you read, you'll see
just how helpful math can be.

Let's get started. Jump right in!
Turn the page, and let's begin!

Multiplex drove his tow truck down Monster Town Road. He sang a song.

"I can fix you up
if your car breaks down.
Call Multiplex Towing
in Monster Town."

Multiplex drove home to the Math Monsters' castle. He jumped out of his truck.

"My job is great," he said. "I love towing cars."

What kind of job do you want to have when you grow up?

5

"How many cars did you tow?" asked Mina.

"None," said Multiplex. "I got a call for help, but I did not find the car."

"What do you mean?" asked Mina.

"I got a call from a driver with a flat tire," said Multiplex. "He told me his car was on the side of the road next to a big green tree. I looked and looked, but I could not find him."

Why do you think Multiplex did not find the driver?

"I know what is wrong," said Split. "There are so many big green trees on Monster Town Road. How can you know which tree he was next to?"

"Maybe we can put up some signs along the road," said Addison. "What kind of signs?" asked Multiplex.

"Number signs," said Addison.

How can putting up number signs help?

"If we put up number signs along the road, drivers can tell us what number they are near," said Addison. "Then it will be easy to find them."

"Our number signs can measure how many monster meters someone is from the castle," said Split.

"We can start here at the castle with zero," said Multiplex.

The monsters measured 1 monster meter away from the castle. They put up the next sign. It was the number 1.

"One monster meter from the castle," said Split.

Addison put up the next sign. "Two monster meters from the castle," he said.

They kept going with number signs for monster meters 3, 4, 5, 6, and 7.

What will the next sign be?

"This is monster meter 8," said Addison. "I am getting tired."

"Monster Town Road is 100 monster meters long!" said Split. "We still have a lot of work to do."

"We cannot make one hundred signs," said Mina. "We do not have that many sign cards left."

"How many cards do we have?" asked Multiplex.

"We only have ten more," said Mina. "We can only make ten more signs."

"How can we get to 100 with ten signs?" asked Multiplex.

How can the monsters reach 100 monster meters using only ten signs?

13

Addison wrote 10 on a card.

"Let's count by tens," he said. "We can put up signs every 10 monster meters."

Addison made more signs.

Mina read, "10, 20, 30, 40, 50."
"What other signs do we need
to reach 100?" asked Multiplex.

What other signs do the monsters need to make?

Mina said, "60, 70, 80, 90, and 100. I will put these signs along the road every 10 monster meters."

She flew off to put them along the road.

Multiplex felt happy as he got
into his truck. Soon his phone rang.

"I need help," said the caller.
"My car just broke down."

"I can help you," said Multiplex,
"but I must ask you something first."

*What do you think
Multiplex will ask
the driver?*

17

"Do you see a number sign by the road?"
asked Multiplex.

"I am standing next to one," said the driver.
"It says 20."

"I know where to find you — at monster meter 20. I will be right over," said Multiplex.

Do you think Multiplex will find the driver?

"I have found you," said Multiplex, "right at monster meter 20."

Multiplex got out of his truck and fixed the tire.

A little later, Mina called. She said, "I see another car that needs help."

"Where is it?" asked Multiplex.

"It is near monster meter 50," she said, "but not right next to it."

What else could Multiplex ask to help him find the car?

21

"Is the car between the signs that say 40 and 50?" asked Multiplex.

"No," said Mina. "It is between the signs that say 50 and 60."

"I can find the car now," said Multiplex.

Multiplex drove up. He said,
"Our number signs really work.
Now it is easy to find the people
who need my help."

He sang his song.
"I can fix you up
if your car breaks down.
Call Multiplex Towing
in Monster Town."

*Do you ever see
number signs on
the road? What
do they tell you?*

ACTIVITIES

Page 5 Talk with children about different jobs people have that help others in the community.

Page 7 Demonstrate the need for details when giving directions about location. Ask children to cover their eyes while you hide a small, familiar item in the room. Ask one child to follow your clues to find it. At first, make the clues general. For example, say, "over there." Then give more specific directions, like "under the green chair." Have children give you specific directions.

Page 9 Explore ways that numbers can provide accurate information. For example, the number in a street address tells exactly where someone lives. The number on a scale tells someone's exact weight.

Pages 11, 13, 15 Use a meter stick or make your own number line with numbers from 0 to 100. Most meter sticks highlight multiples of 10. You can do the same on your number line. Use it to compare counting to 100 by ones to counting by tens.

Pages 17, 19, 21 Talk with children about how monster meters are like the numbers on the meter stick or number line you have created. Use a model car to demonstrate the situations Multiplex faces, finding cars at monster meter 20 and between 50 and 60.

Page 23 On your next road trip, discuss the number signs along the road, such as mile markers, kilometer markers, speed limits, route signs, and exit numbers. Point out that there is even a number line right in your car — the speedometer!